ISBN 978-1-5279-1501-5
PIBN 10907381

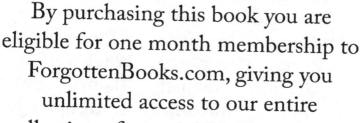

FARMERS' BULLETIN No. 2107

**DEFENSE
AGAINST**

Radioactive Fallout
on the farm

CONTENTS

If we were attacked with nuclear weapons (atomic or hydrogen bombs), you, the American farmer, would be counted on to supply the food and fiber needed to keep the economy going. One of the problems you might face in doing this important job is radioactive fallout.

This bulletin contains the recommendations of scientists, engineers, public health officials, Civil Defense authorities, and other specialists. You may not find here all the information that you would like to have on protection against fallout. Study of the effect of radioactive fallout on agriculture is a continuing project. Some of the recommendations in this bulletin may have to be changed in the light of future research.

In the event of enemy attack, first provide for your own safety and that of your family and neighbors. To do this, you may initially have to ignore your livestock, your crops, and your land. Your best protection from fallout is to remain indoors, preferably in a basement or cellar, and to avoid contact with contaminated objects. When in doubt, seek shelter. Authorities will make every effort to let you know when it is safe to come out of shelter.

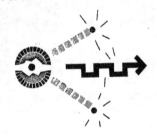

Washington, D. C.   Issued June 1957

2

FALLOUT: *BACKGROUND*

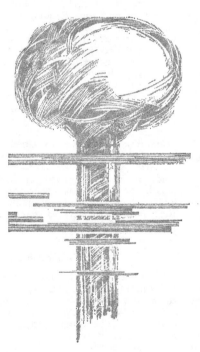

Most Americans know about the destructive power of atomic and hydrogen bombs and other nuclear weapons. The explosive power of the atomic bombs used in World War II was equivalent to about 20,000 tons of TNT. Since then, bombs have been developed that have explosive power equivalent to millions of tons of TNT.

An enemy attack with a nuclear weapon could cause radioactive contamination many miles downwind from the target area. Radioactive particles produced by the bomb may give off destructive rays, which, in certain situations, can injure—or kill—human beings and animals, and can make farm lands and crops dangerous to use. These particles are called radioactive fallout.

Fallout could settle anywhere—even in the most remote parts of the country. If large industrial centers were bombed with hydrogen weapons, it is likely that small towns and rural areas in the downwind path would be endangered.

Fallout may or may not be visible, and the radiation from the active elements can be detected only by special instruments. Because of this, you will be notified through regular Civil Defense channels when your lands lie within the path of harmful radioactive contamination.

3

There is a defense against fallout—on the farm and in the home. The following questions and answers will help you to understand the nature of fallout, and, in the event of enemy attack, will help you protect yourself from it.

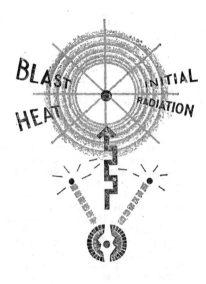

What is radioactivity?

It is a process whereby certain elements disintegrate, and in so doing release one or more types of powerful rays.

Radioactivity is nothing new. All living things are constantly exposed to small amounts of radiation. Cosmic rays from space continually pass through our bodies. We breathe and eat radioactive materials that occur naturally in the soil, water, and air. We also are exposed to radiation when we have X-ray examinations. But explosions of nuclear bombs produce large amounts of radioactive elements that can affect the health of human beings and animals. NOTE: *In the case of United States nuclear tests, precautions are taken to protect the public against the hazard of fallout.*

What happens when a nuclear bomb explodes?

The explosion of an atomic or hydrogen bomb is accompanied by *blast, heat, initial radiation, and residual radiation.* The first three occur almost instantaneously with the explosion, and are destructive at the target area and for some miles around. The fourth—residual radiation—has a delayed and longer effect, and may be dangerous over a considerably larger area.

What is fallout?

Fallout is the term used to describe radioactive particles, produced by nuclear explosions, that fall to earth from the upper air. When the bomb explodes close to the earth, large quantities of soil, rock, and debris are drawn up into the ascending cloud. After mixing with the highly radioactive material, particles fall back to earth and produce radioactive contamination. Some of the particles fall close to the point of the explosion, while others may drift downwind for many miles before settling to earth.

A bomb exploded high in the air does not produce immediate serious fallout because there is no heavy debris taken up into the cloud to bring the radioactive material down to earth. The radioactive particles tend to remain suspended for days, months or years in the upper atmosphere where much of the radioactivity is lost harmlessly before settling to earth.

Why is fallout dangerous?

If an area is highly contaminated by fallout, the radiation may be a threat to human beings, animals, and crops. Fallout can also contaminate food, water, buildings, yards, and fields, and make them unsafe to use for certain periods.

Some of the rays can penetrate the body and cause serious internal damage. Others, while not capable of deep penetration, can burn the skin. Some of the radioactive chemical elements in the fallout, such as radioactive strontium and radioactive iodine, can cause serious internal radiation damage if taken into the body in sufficiently large quantities.

To understand the nature of fallout, it is necessary to know that fallout particles contain a mixture of long-lived and short-lived materials, each of which decays at a specific rate. Scientists usually measure the decay rate by the half-life of the material. The half-life is the time required for one-half, or 50 percent, of a given amount of a specific material to decay. Radioactive strontium is among the most important of the long-lived group. Radioactive iodine is an example of an important relatively short-lived substance.

Chemically, radioactive strontium is similar to calcium. After it enters the body, it tends to collect in the bones. It has a half-life of about 28 years, and large amounts of it in the body can cause bone cancer, and can damage tissue.

Radioactive iodine has a half-life of about 8 days, and therefore is not dangerous for as long a time as radioactive strontium. After it enters the body, it tends to collect in the thyroid gland. If too much of it is present in the body, it may cause cancer of the thyroid gland and otherwise seriously damage the thyroid cells.

Small concentrations of radioactive strontium and radioactive iodine are not dangerous to most persons if exposure is not prolonged.

Fallout can be a serious hazard to communities that are miles beyond the areas affected by the explosion. During a 1954 test at the Eniwetok Proving Grounds in the Pacific, the area where fallout would have seriously threatened nearly all the lives of persons who took no protective measures extended about 140 miles downwind from the point of explosion, and was up to 20 miles in width.

What determines the size of the fallout area?

The extent and location of a fallout area are determined by—

1. Altitude of the bomb burst.
2. Power and design of the bomb.
3. Size of the fallout particles.
4. Atmospheric conditions—air currents and the direction and speed of the winds, particularly those at 10,000 to 80,000 feet.
5. Snow and rain.
6. The nature of the ground surface.

Because of the variety of factors, it is not possible to estimate accurately the fallout hazard in advance. However, the area of probable fallout and

---

FOR FURTHER INFORMATION . . .

Civil Defense Household First-Aid Kit.—Tells what you should have in a home emergency kit and how to use each item.

Between You and Disaster.—Tells how to select a 7-day food supply for use in event of disaster.

Before Disaster Strikes.—Gives information on maintaining sanitary conditions in the home during the first few days after an enemy attack.

Facts About the H-Bomb.—Describes dangers of the H-bomb and tells how to combat them.

You may obtain copies of these publications from your nearest Civil Defense office or from the Federal Civil Defense Administration, Battle Creek, Mich.

the speed with which fallout will arrive can be estimated. Such forecasts are to be released by the Weather Bureau and will be available to Civil Defense authorities.

After a bomb is exploded close to the ground, the large radioactive cloud rises to a high level in the atmosphere. The particles are acted upon by the wind. Some of the particles are carried upwind, downwind, and crosswind, in the area of the target. Others are carried long distances downwind. Strong winds may spread fallout over wide areas.

Raindrops and snowflakes passing through contaminated air collect fallout. Particles that would normally spread over wide areas during dry weather quickly come to earth.

Hills, valleys, and slopes probably have no great effect on the distribution of fallout, but large mountains and ridges receive a high concentration of fallout on the side facing the surface wind. Wherever possible, radiation intensity should be checked in the local areas.

How long is fallout dangerous?

The greatest hazard exists during the early hours following the explosion, when the radiation is very intense. The hazard decreases with the passage of time because radioactive materials decay, and as they decay the intensity of radiation decreases.

The particles reaching the ground soon after the burst are highly radioactive, while those that remain in the air for longer periods lose much of their radioactivity by decay before they settle to earth. Twenty-four hours after an explosion the average per-hour rate of radiation of a given particle is about 2 percent of the rate 1 hour after the explosion. But even this amount of radiation can be dangerous if there is a heavy concentration of fallout. Long half-life radioactive substances, such as strontium 90, are referred to on page 5.

How can I protect my family and myself from radiation?

The effect of radiation is in proportion to the period of exposure. Limit your exposure to it.

You can limit exposure by staying in an adequate shelter. Several feet of earth or concrete provide excellent

shielding from radiation. The walls of an ordinary frame house give some protection.

You can also limit exposure by getting away from the source of radiation. Radiation is absorbed in the air, and is significantly reduced a few hundred feet from the source. (See "Fallout: More Pointers on Protection," p. 14.)

How will I know if fallout is coming?

In the event of an enemy attack, Civil Defense officials and other authorized personnel will issue instructions by all available means of communication. If the radio and TV stations you normally listen to go off the air, attempt to tune in another station. If you cannot receive another station, try to get 640 or 1240, the CONELRAD Civil Defense frequencies, on your radio dial. You

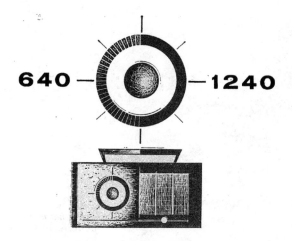

640 — **1240**

may not be within the effective range of a CONELRAD station. In that event, follow whatever instructions you have received from your local, county, or State Civil Defense.

Later you will receive information based on the findings of aerial or ground monitors who will conduct surveys in the areas involved. The monitors will measure the radiation from the fallout with suitable instruments to determine what further precautions, if any, should be taken.

Remember! Fallout is odorless and may be invisible. It can be measured only with proper instruments. However, after an atomic attack, dust clouds or unusual dust concentrations in the atmosphere should be assumed to be radioactive until they have been officially surveyed with instruments and found not to be radioactive.

Should I have
a Geiger counter or some
other device to detect fallout?

You would not find a Geiger counter useful because the instruments commonly available are designed for

such use as uranium prospecting and are not satisfactory for measuring dangerous levels of fallout.

Even the proper instruments are of no value except when used by experienced persons who are qualified to interpret the readings.

FALLOUT: *LIVESTOCK*

How will fallout affect unprotected livestock—that is, animals in fields, pastures, and other open areas?

Fallout may be dangerous to cattle, sheep, horses, pigs, and other livestock as well as to human beings. Animals can suffer skin burns if fallout settles in the coat. If animals drink fallout in their water or eat it in pasture grass or commercial feed, the radiation may cause serious internal injuries. External radiation or surface contamination emits rays capable of penetrating deep into the body and may result in total body exposure.

If you receive ample warning that fallout is coming, you can take certain precautions to protect your livestock and reduce losses. But once fallout occurs, you should not attempt to protect livestock unless Civil Defense officials tell you that it is safe to do so.

How will fallout affect sheltered livestock?

Livestock housed in barns and other farm buildings during fallout stand a better chance of surviving the effects of radiation than those that are not sheltered. A reasonably well-built shelter prevents fallout from settling on the animals' bodies and may reduce the intensity of external radiation. It also protects against the animals' eating contaminated food.

*What is the best way
to protect livestock from fallout?*

Move them indoors as soon as possible, and keep them off contaminated feed and water. If you do not have adequate facilities to house livestock, put them near farm buildings, in a yard, or in a tree-sheltered field.

Get your dairy cattle under cover first. If they eat fallout, or drink it in water, some of the radioactive material will be in their manure and urine, and some will be in their milk.

*What water and feed can
I give livestock after fallout?*

Caution: Do not allow your animals to go without water and feed too long. It is better to keep them alive on contaminated water and feed than to let them die of thirst and hunger.

Water and feed become contaminated if they are exposed to fallout.

Water from a covered well, tank, or cistern, or from a freely running spring, should be safe. If possible, use water from a covered well.

Pond water is less safe, but, if necessary, it can be used a few days after fallout has occurred.

To prevent contamination from fallout, do not add water to tanks or cisterns, except water from a properly protected well or spring, until the water originally present is used.

Give your livestock feed that has not been exposed to fallout. If the particles settle on hay, silage, or a stack of feedbags, they will contaminate only the outer portions. You can remove the outer layers or bags, and use the inside feed that is unaffected. Do not handle contaminated feed until told by the Civil Defense authorities that it is safe to do so, and be sure to follow the precautions they may recommend.

Farmers will be notified if authorities measuring concentrations of fallout consider forage growing in an area to be harmful.

You may have to give cows contaminated feed if no other feed is available. Although the milk from these cows may not be usable for a brief period, once the cows are back on clean feed the amount of radioactive materials in their milk will progressively diminish. Civil Defense authorities will measure fallout in affected areas and warn farmers when milk is unsafe.

*What can I do
with contaminated feed?*

You may be able to feed it to livestock eventually. Because of radioactive decay, even dangerously contaminated feed may be safe to use after a period of storage. How long feed should be stored depends on such factors as the age, amount, and concentration of the fission products. Area monitors will notify farmers of these factors through regular Civil Defense channels. Long half-life radioactive substances, such as strontium 90, are referred to on page 5.

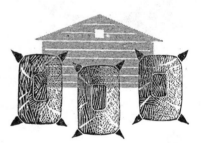

*Should dairy cows
receive special treatment?*

Yes. Since radioactive materials can accumulate in milk, which will be a very critical product during an emergency, you should make a special effort to protect cows from fallout.

Give cows preferred shelter and

clean feed and water. If you can, milk them before fallout occurs. You may not be able to do so for a day or two afterwards. Reduce amounts of water and concentrated feed, and, if practicable, put cows and calves together; the calves can suckle and reduce the discomfort of full udders.

What measures should be taken to protect poultry?

Measures for protecting poultry are the same as those recommended for other farm animals. Flocks housed in concrete buildings would be better protected from fallout than those housed in wooden buildings.

Radioactive materials might show up in the eggs if hens eat contaminated feed. But most of the radioactive strontium will collect in the shells; very little will collect in the yolk and in the white.

What animal food products are safe to market after fallout?

You will receive specific instructions from the Civil Defense authorities based on the amount of fallout received. *Do not destroy any animal food products unless spoilage has made them inedible.* Contaminated food products may be safe for consumption if they can be stored for a period of time to allow the radioactivity to decay.

What do I do if animals die from fallout?

Some of your animals may be affected so severely from fallout that they will die in a few days or weeks after being exposed. Others will be unthrifty; they may have to be slaughtered. *Do not slaughter any of your livestock unless you are told to do so by Civil Defense or agricultural authorities.*

If animals die from fallout, you can dispose of the bodies by burial. These carcasses usually are not dangerous to surviving animals. Special instructions for your protection while handling contaminated carcasses may be issued by Civil Defense authorities, depending on the amount of contamination present.

Is it possible to decontaminate livestock and farm buildings that have been exposed to fallout?

If there is fallout on the animals' skins, much of the radioactivity can be washed off. Civil Defense authorities may advise you to hose down animals and to clean stables, barns, and other farm buildings. They will also tell you when it is safe to do these things. In handling animals, take proper precautions to prevent contaminating yourself. Cleaning or disinfecting buildings will not destroy radioactivity.

Caution: Before hosing down animals or cleaning buildings, a thorough check should be made of possible radiation hazards.

FALLOUT: LAND AND CROPS

What are the main consequences of heavy concentrations of fallout on crop and pasture lands?

1. Farm workers may not be able to manage and cultivate land safely for some time because of radiation hazard.

2. It may not be advisable to permit animals to graze because of the danger of internal and external radiation.

3. Radioactive materials that are deposited on the edible portions of plants or absorbed through the roots are a potential long-term hazard to human beings and animals.

How long would fallout affect cultivated and noncultivated lands?

It would depend on the abundance and type of radioactive materials in a given area.

Short- and medium-lived materials would decay rapidly; the principal danger from them would be external radiation. Although the hazard may be reduced in days or weeks after fallout, contamination should be checked by radiological monitoring.

Radioactive strontium—a long-lived material—could affect soils and plants for decades. Since it is chemically similar to calcium, it would be absorbed by plants that require calcium. Plants growing in soils deficient in calcium would absorb more radioactive strontium than those growing in soils abundant in calcium, other conditions being equal.

Cultivated land probably would remain hazardous a shorter time than range land. Cultivation would cover

11

most of the radioactive particles. Also, soil erosion is greater on cultivated land; some radioactive particles would be carried away.

Are there treatments for reducing the fallout hazard on land?

Yes. You can treat lands to reduce the fallout hazard after external radiation levels are low enough to go outdoors and work. One possible treatment is to leach porous soils with water. Other treatments include: Intensive liming of strongly acid and moderately acid soils, adding large amounts of decomposable organic matter to the soil, and plowing deep the surface layer of the soil. *Note:* Selection of the proper treatment requires the advice of a soil scientist.

It probably would be uneconomical to decontaminate range lands.

Would fallout permanently affect pasture grass?

A heavy deposit of fallout would spread short-lived and long-lived radioactive particles on the pasture. The existing growth would be affected by particles that have fallen on the exposed portions of the plants; succeeding growths, following grazing or mowing, would be affected internally from the long-lived radioactive materials absorbed from the soil by the roots. There probably would be no visible injury to the plants from the radiation.

Could I ever use contaminated pasture grass?

If fallout is light, the pasture might be usable immediately.

If fallout is heavy on soils that have a low available calcium level, it is advisable to plow soil deep, lime, and replant; on soils that have a high available calcium level, mow and discard existing growth. Another alternative is to allow livestock to graze on contaminated pasture, and use meat and milk under the supervision of the radiological defense supervisor. This may be the only available course during an emergency in order to keep the livestock alive. *Note:* Determining the best course requires the advice of a soil scientist.

Once it is safe to work the land, a periodic check on pasture and produce in affected areas will provide the best guide as to their use.

Will fallout affect my system of farming?

It could. If your land is seriously contaminated, it may be necessary to change to nonfood crops or to food crops that do not absorb large amounts of fallout from the soil. Alfalfa, clover, soybeans, and leafy vegetables would have a tendency to absorb long-lived radioactive strontium, while cereal grains, potatoes, and fruits would not.

Would fallout reduce the economic productivity of crop and pasture lands?

Yes, it might reduce such productivity in several ways: (1) Crop and soil management would be impeded because of the danger of external radiation; (2) crops would become contaminated and unmarketable; and (3) some lower-yielding crops that do not absorb large quantities of fallout would be substituted for higher-yielding crops that do.

When could I use water in an exposed field?

Water in an exposed field would be contaminated; the hazard in using

in the water, reducing the contamination at the surface. If the water were being constantly replenished from an uncontaminated source, radioactivity would be diluted rapidly.

What are the effects of fallout on growing vegetables?

Growing vegetables that are exposed to heavy fallout may become highly radioactive. Leaves, pods, and fruits are immediately contaminated upon contact with the radioactive particles. Roots and tubers are affected only if they absorb long-lived materials, such as radioactive strontium, from the soil. Underground vegetables may become affected if they touch contaminated surface soil during harvest. *Most vegetables would be marketable, and should not be destroyed without testing for radioactivity.*

What are the effects of fallout on growing fruit, including green fruit and ripe fruit?

If fallout is heavy, ripe, thin-skinned fruits may be lost because of the personal hazard involved in harvesting them. Thick-skinned fruits that do not have to be picked immediately and are peeled before eating can be

radioactivity before and after harvest.

What effect would fallout have on alfalfa and other feed crops?

Existing growths of alfalfa and other feed crops might not be usable because of radiation hazard. Radioactivity would be less in subsequent growths. What you should do depends on the calcium level of your soil. *Acid soils that have a low available calcium level:* A new planting should be made after the original planting is plowed deep, and lime is applied. *Soils that have a high available calcium level:* If a radiation survey indicates that the contamination level is high enough to require it, the existing growth should be mowed and discarded, and only succeeding growths used.

Would fallout limit the use of plants for human food?

It depends on the extent of the radioactivity.

Leafy vegetables, such as lettuce, should not be eaten unless they are thoroughly washed, and are known to be free of hazardous amounts of radioactivity.

What special precautions should be taken for workers in the fields?

Everyone should remain indoors until the danger from fallout has diminished. When you are advised by Civil Defense officials that it is safe to work outdoors, you may be asked to take certain precautions, such as wearing boots, coat, hat, and gloves. If you work with livestock, touch them as little as possible; fallout may be on their backs.

13

FALLOUT:

MORE POINTERS ON PROTECTION

What you can do now . . .

●*Determine what shelter area will best protect your family and yourself.*
●Learn official Civil Defense action signals, and what to do when you hear them.
●Prepare your home: (*a*) Obtain a Civil Defense disaster first-aid kit. (*b*) Learn how to use it. (*c*) Practice fire-safe housekeeping. (*d*) Learn to fight small fires. (*e*) Maintain a 7-day emergency supply of food and water at all times, and store it in the basement. (*f*) Equip the most protected place you can find in or near your home for a shelter. (*g*) Make a list of the things you would need during a stay of several days in the shelter; place as many of these as possible in the shelter. (*h*) Know how to practice emergency sanitation measures if necessary.
●Memorize the CONELRAD frequencies of 640 and 1240 on the AM radio dial. (See pp. 6 and 7.) These are the stations that will carry official information and instructions in an emergency. If possible, obtain a battery radio; the explosion may cause a power breakdown.
●Plan an emergency water supply and a sewage disposal method for your home shelter area that do not depend on outside electric power. Remember, a spring or deep well may be useless if the pump depends on public power supplies.

If you have a few hours' warning . . .

●*Make arrangements for the safety of your family and yourself.* Have about a 2 weeks' supply of food in the house.
●Bring feed into buildings, or cover it with tarpaulin if it is left outdoors.
●Store as much water as possible for livestock, especially if the water is coming from ponds or streams or through water mains. Cover wells and rainbarrels.
●Move farm machinery and equipment indoors or store them near the farm house and keep them covered.

If you have a few months' warning . . .

If the Government is able to give the public a few months' warning that an atomic attack is likely, here are some things that you can do:
●Put your silage pits and hay stack near buildings and cover them with tarpaulins.
●Keep your well clean and covered. Put some rainwater barrels and other

containers ·near buildings; ·fill them
regularly with clean water and keep
them covered.

●Store seed and grain in weather-
proof buildings.

●Stock up on packaged, canned, and
bottled foods.

●Have a satisfactory storage space
for fuel.

)N

) These
y official
s in an
:n a bat-
y cause a

: supply
:hod for
: do not
: power.
we'l may
:ads on

:ning ...

:afity of
e about
:s house.
or cover
:tdoors.
possible
:e water
:ams or
:r wells

:: equip-
:=ar the
:=ed.

:ing ...

: :o give
::rning
:.v, here
: :o:
:r stack
:=n with

:vered.
:.! other

This publication has been prepared by the U. S. Department of Agriculture in cooperation with the Atomic Energy Commission, the Federal Civil Defense Administration, and the U. S. Public Health Service. It deals with radioactive contamination conditions that may exist following the explosion of nuclear weapons during war. It does not relate to conditions that result from the testing of continental nuclear weapons. In such testing, the amount of radioactive contamination is kept within limits considered to be compatible with public health.

U. S. GOVERNMENT PRINTING OFFICE: 1957

For sale by the Superintendent of Documents, U. S. Government Printing Office
Washington 25, D. C. - Price 10 cents

CPSIA information can be obtained
at www.ICGtesting.com
Printed in the USA
BVHW072123231118
533618BV00054B/3470/P